Windows Forensics: Basic Concepts and Techniques

By

Issa Ngoie

CONTENTS

1. **Overview of Digital Forensics and Windows Forensics**: This chapter provides an introduction to digital forensics and focuses on the basics of Windows forensics, including the various types of digital evidence that can be recovered from Windows operating systems.

2. **Windows File Systems**: This chapter provides an overview of the Windows file system, including the differences between NTFS and FAT file systems, their structures, and how to analyze them for forensic purposes.

3. **Collecting and Analyzing Windows Artifacts:** This chapter covers the types of artifacts that can be collected from Windows operating systems, including file system artifacts, registry artifacts, and user and system artifacts.

4. **Windows Forensic Tools and Techniques:** This chapter provides an overview of the various tools and techniques used in Windows forensics, including imaging, hashing, analysis tools, and memory analysis tools.

5. **Case Studies:** This chapter presents case studies that demonstrate the application of Windows forensics concepts and techniques in real-world scenarios, including investigating computer misuse, data theft, and employee misconduct.

INTRODUCTION

The Windows registry was introduced in Windows 3.1 in 1992 as a centralized database for storing system and application settings. Prior to the registry, settings were stored in various configuration files scattered throughout the file system, making it difficult to manage and maintain.

The first version of the Windows registry was called Registration Database (REG.DAT) and contained a limited number of settings. It was stored in the root directory of the system drive and was loaded into memory during system startup.

With the introduction of Windows 95 in 1995, the registry was completely overhauled and became an essential part of the operating system. The new registry was based on a hierarchical structure, similar to a file system, and contained separate sections for different components of the operating system and installed applications. This made it easier to manage and organize the settings and allowed for more efficient access and querying.

Windows 98 and Windows 2000 introduced further improvements to the registry, including support for Unicode, which allowed for the use of non-Latin characters, and the ability to store larger values and data types.

Windows XP, released in 2001, introduced additional security measures to the registry, including access control lists (ACLs) and the ability to audit registry changes. These features helped prevent unauthorized access and modification of registry settings.

Since then, the Windows registry has continued to evolve, with new features and improvements added in each new version of Windows. Despite its importance to the functioning of the operating system and installed applications, the registry can become cluttered and fragmented over time, which can lead to performance issues and other problems. As a result, registry cleaning and optimization tools have become popular among Windows users.

CHAPTER I : OVERVIEW OF DIGITAL FORENSICS AND WINDOWS FORENSICS

Digital forensics is the process of collecting, analyzing, and preserving electronic data to support an investigation or legal proceeding. It involves identifying, preserving, analyzing, and presenting electronic evidence in a manner that is admissible in court. Digital forensics can be applied to a wide range of devices and platforms, including computers, mobile devices, and network systems.

Windows forensics is a subset of digital forensics that focuses on the collection and analysis of electronic evidence from Windows operating systems. Windows is the most widely used operating system in the world, which makes it a frequent target for cyberattacks and other malicious activities. Windows forensics involves the identification, acquisition, analysis, and reporting of digital evidence from Windows systems.

The basics of Windows forensics include understanding the Windows file system, the various types of artifacts that can be collected from Windows systems, and the tools and techniques used to collect and analyze digital evidence. The

Windows file system includes the NTFS and FAT file systems, which have different structures and store data differently.

Artifacts that can be collected from Windows systems include file system artifacts, registry artifacts, and user and system artifacts. File system artifacts include information about files, directories, and file metadata, such as file size, dates, and permissions. Registry artifacts include information stored in the Windows registry, such as application settings, user profiles, and system configurations. User and system artifacts include information about user activity, network connections, and system processes.

Windows forensics tools and techniques include imaging, hashing, analysis tools, and memory analysis tools. Imaging involves creating a bit-by-bit copy of a disk or other storage device, which can be used to preserve and analyze digital evidence. Hashing is the process of creating a unique digital fingerprint of a file or other data, which can be used to verify the integrity of the data.

Analysis tools used in Windows forensics include tools for file system analysis, registry analysis, and internet history analysis. Memory analysis tools are used to analyze the contents of a computer's RAM, which can provide valuable information about running processes, network connections, and other system activity.

Windows operating systems store a wide range of digital evidence that can be collected and analyzed for forensic purposes. Some of the most common types of digital evidence that can be recovered from Windows systems include:

1. **File system artifacts**: File system artifacts include file metadata, such as file name, size, date and time of creation, last access, and modification, as well as file content. Windows file systems, such as NTFS and FAT, store this information in various data structures, including Master File Table (MFT) and File Allocation Table (FAT).
2. **Registry artifacts**: The Windows registry is a hierarchical database that stores settings and configurations for Windows and its applications. Registry artifacts include information about user accounts, installed software, system configuration, and other system settings. This information

can be analyzed to determine user activity, system changes, and other relevant information.

3. **Internet history**: Internet history artifacts include browsing history, cookies, and other temporary files stored by web browsers, such as Internet Explorer, Edge, Firefox, and Chrome. These artifacts can reveal the websites visited by a user, the search terms used, and other online activity.

4. **User and system artifacts:** User and system artifacts include information about user activity, network connections, and system processes. These artifacts can be found in various locations, such as event logs, system files, and other system databases.

5. **Email artifacts**: Email artifacts include email messages, attachments, and metadata, such as sender, recipient, date and time, and subject. Email artifacts can be found in email clients, such as Microsoft Outlook, and web-based email services, such as Gmail and Yahoo.

6. **Mobile device artifacts**: Windows mobile devices, such as Windows phones and tablets, store digital evidence that can be analyzed for forensic purposes. Mobile device artifacts include call logs, text messages, contacts, and other data stored on the device.

7.

CONCLUSION

Windows operating systems store a wide range of digital evidence that can be recovered and analyzed for forensic purposes. Understanding the types of digital evidence that can be found on Windows systems is essential for conducting effective forensic investigations.

One real-world scenario where digital forensics was used involved the investigation of a cyber attack on a financial institution.

The financial institution's network had been compromised, and confidential customer information had been stolen. The institution engaged a team of digital forensic investigators to determine the cause of the breach and the extent of the damage.

The investigators began by collecting and analyzing data from the institution's network devices, servers, and workstations. They used specialized forensic tools to analyze log files, network traffic, and system artifacts.

Through this analysis, the investigators were able to determine that the attackers had gained access to the network through a phishing email that had been sent to an employee. The email contained a malicious attachment that, when opened, installed malware on the employee's computer.

The malware then enabled the attackers to move laterally through the network, eventually gaining access to the database containing customer information. The attackers then exfiltrated the data to a remote server, where it could be accessed and sold on the dark web.

The investigators were able to identify the attackers by tracing the IP address used to access the remote server and by analyzing other indicators of compromise. They worked with law enforcement to apprehend the attackers and recover the stolen data.

In this scenario, digital forensics was essential in identifying the cause of the breach, the extent of the damage, and the perpetrators. It also helped the financial institution take steps to prevent similar breaches from occurring in the future.

QUESTIONS AND ANSWERS

Q: What is digital forensics? A: Digital forensics is the process of collecting, analyzing, and preserving electronic data for use as evidence in legal investigations or proceedings.

Q: What is Windows forensics? A: Windows forensics is a specialized area of digital forensics that involves the collection and analysis of electronic data from Windows operating systems and related applications.

Q: What types of digital evidence can be recovered from Windows systems? A: Digital evidence that can be recovered from Windows systems includes file system artifacts, registry artifacts, internet history, user and system artifacts, email artifacts, and mobile device artifacts.

Q: What are some common tools used in Windows forensics? A: Some common tools used in Windows forensics include EnCase, FTK (Forensic Toolkit), Autopsy, and Sleuth Kit.

Q: What are some best practices for conducting Windows forensics investigations? A: Best practices for conducting

Windows forensics investigations include maintaining a proper chain of custody, preserving original evidence, minimizing data alteration or destruction, and ensuring that all procedures and methods used comply with relevant legal and ethical standards.

Q: What are some challenges associated with Windows forensics? A: Challenges associated with Windows forensics include the complexity and size of the Windows operating system and related applications, the constantly evolving nature of digital technology, and the potential for data corruption or loss during the investigation process.

Q: What are some potential applications of Windows forensics? A: Windows forensics can be used in a variety of applications, including criminal investigations, corporate investigations, incident response, and data recovery. It can also be used to investigate cybercrime, insider threats, and intellectual property theft.

QUESTIONS

1. What is the purpose of digital forensics?
2. How is digital evidence collected and preserved in digital forensics investigations?
3. What are some examples of digital evidence that can be recovered from Windows systems?
4. What are some common challenges associated with conducting Windows forensics investigations?
5. How do tools like EnCase and FTK assist in Windows forensics investigations?
6. What are some best practices for conducting a successful Windows forensics investigation?
7. In what types of legal cases might Windows forensics be useful?
8. What role does chain of custody play in Windows forensics investigations?
9. What are some potential consequences of mishandling digital evidence in a Windows forensics investigation?
10. How has the evolution of Windows operating systems impacted the practice of digital forensics?

CHAPTER II: WINDOWS FILE SYSTEMS

The Windows file system is the underlying structure that organizes and stores files on a Windows operating system. There are two primary types of file systems used in Windows: FAT (File Allocation Table) and NTFS (New Technology File System).

FAT is an older file system that is commonly used on removable storage devices such as USB drives and SD cards. It is a relatively simple file system that uses a table to track the location of files on the storage device. FAT has several limitations, including a maximum file size of 4GB and a lack of support for file permissions and security features.

NTFS is a newer file system that is used on most modern Windows operating systems. It provides advanced features such as support for file compression, encryption, and permissions. NTFS uses a Master File Table (MFT) to store information about files on the file system, including the location of the file, its size, and its access permissions.

The Windows file system organizes files into directories, which are also known as folders. Directories can contain files, as well as other directories, allowing for a hierarchical organization of files on the file system.

In addition to regular files and directories, the Windows file system also contains system files, which are used by the operating system to perform various tasks. These system files include device drivers, configuration files, and DLLs (Dynamic Link Libraries) that are used to provide functionality to installed applications.

The Windows file system can also contain deleted files, which may be recoverable through the use of specialized forensic tools. When a file is deleted, its data is not immediately removed from the file system, but rather the file system marks the space occupied by the file as available for reuse. This means that with the proper tools and techniques, deleted files may be recovered from the file system.

Overall, the Windows file system is a complex and sophisticated system that plays a critical role in the functioning of the Windows operating system and related applications. Understanding the structure and organization of the file system is an essential component of conducting successful Windows forensics investigations.

NTFS and **FAT** are two file systems used in Windows operating systems. While they both serve the same purpose of organizing and managing data, they differ in their structures, capabilities, and forensic analysis.

Structure:

NTFS (New Technology File System) is a more advanced and complex file system than FAT (File Allocation Table). NTFS uses a Master File Table (MFT) to keep track of files and directories. The MFT is a database-like structure that stores metadata such as file names, file attributes, and file permissions. NTFS supports larger file sizes, file compression, encryption, and has better data recovery features.

FAT, on the other hand, uses a File Allocation Table to keep track of the location of files on the disk. FAT has a simpler structure and is commonly used on removable **storage devices such as USB drives and SD cards.**

Forensic Analysis:

Forensic analysis of NTFS and FAT file systems requires different techniques and tools. In NTFS, the MFT is the primary source of file information. Forensic investigators can use tools such as EnCase, FTK, and Autopsy to extract data from the MFT and recover deleted files.

In FAT, the File Allocation Table is used to keep track of files. The FAT file system does not have a built-in journaling feature, making it more challenging to recover deleted files. However, forensic investigators can use tools such as Scalpel and Foremost to carve data from the file system and recover deleted files.

One real-world scenario where Windows file systems were analyzed involved an investigation of a computer that was suspected of being used for illegal activities.

The computer's file system was imaged, and forensic analysis was performed on the image to identify any suspicious files or activity. The analysis focused on the NTFS file system, which is commonly used on Windows-based computers.

Through the analysis, the investigators were able to identify several suspicious files, including encrypted archives and files with names that suggested they contained illegal content. The investigators used specialized forensic tools to recover the deleted files, and were able to find evidence of illegal activities, including the distribution of child pornography.

The analysis also revealed that the suspect had used various techniques to hide their activity, including renaming files with innocuous names, encrypting files, and deleting files to cover their tracks. However, through the use of forensic techniques, the investigators were able to uncover the suspect's activity and build a case against them.

In this scenario, the analysis of the Windows file system was crucial in identifying evidence of illegal activity and building a case against the suspect. It also demonstrated the importance of using specialized forensic tools to recover deleted or hidden files and uncover suspicious activity on a computer.

QUESTIONS AND ANSWERS

Q: What is the Windows file system? A: The Windows file system is a hierarchical directory structure used by the Windows operating system to organize and store files and folders on a computer's hard drive.

Q: What is the name of the default file system used by Windows? A: The default file system used by Windows is called NTFS (New Technology File System).

Q: What are the advantages of using NTFS over the older FAT file system? A: NTFS offers several advantages over the older FAT file system, including improved performance, enhanced security features, and support for larger file sizes and disk volumes.

Q: What is a file path in Windows? A: A file path in Windows is a unique identifier that specifies the location of a file or folder within the file system. It includes the name of the drive, the path to the directory, and the name of the file or folder.

Q: What is a file extension in Windows? A: A file extension in Windows is a set of characters that follow the last dot in a file name and indicate the type of file it is. For example, .docx indicates a Microsoft Word document, while .mp3 indicates an audio file.

Q: What is a file attribute in Windows? A: A file attribute in Windows is a characteristic of a file that describes its properties, such as its read-only status, hidden status, or archive status.

Q: What is a file permission in Windows? A: A file permission in Windows is a set of rules that determine who can access or modify a file, and what actions they can perform on it. Permissions are set by the owner of the file or by a system administrator.

CHAPTER III: COLLECTING AND ANALYZING WINDOWS ARTIFACTS

An artifact is any piece of data or information that is created, used, or left behind as a result of a digital activity. In the context of digital forensics, an artifact is any trace or piece of evidence that can provide information about a digital device or the activity that took place on that device.

Examples of digital artifacts can include log files, registry keys, browser history, emails, chat logs, documents, images, and other types of digital files. These artifacts can be analyzed to reconstruct digital events, identify user activity, and uncover potential evidence of criminal or malicious behavior.

Digital artifacts can be found on a variety of digital devices, including computers, mobile devices, and other digital storage media. The analysis of digital artifacts is an important aspect of digital forensics and can provide valuable insights into past digital activities.

There are several types of artifacts that can be collected from Windows operating systems. These artifacts can provide valuable information to digital forensic investigators and can help them understand the actions that were performed on the system. Some common types of artifacts that can be collected from Windows operating systems include:

1. **Registry keys**: The Windows registry is a database that contains configuration settings for the operating system and applications installed on the system. Registry keys can provide information about installed software, user activity, and system configurations.
2. **File system artifacts**: The Windows file system contains a wealth of information that can be useful in digital forensics investigations. File system artifacts can include file timestamps, file metadata, and deleted files.
3. Event logs: Windows operating systems generate event logs that can provide information about system activity,

including user logins, application launches, and system errors.

4. **Internet history**: Internet history can be collected from web browsers and can provide information about websites visited, user activity, and downloaded files.

5. **Email artifacts**: Emails and email attachments can be recovered from the Windows operating system and can provide information about user activity, communication patterns, and potentially malicious emails.

6. **Memory artifacts:** Memory can be captured and analyzed to identify running processes, open network connections, and potentially malicious activity.

7. **Prefetch files**: Prefetch files are generated by the Windows operating system to improve the performance of frequently used applications. These files can provide information about which applications were run on the system and when they were run.

8. User activity logs: User activity logs can provide information about user activity, including user logins, file and folder access, and application usage.

It is important to note that the specific artifacts that can be collected will depend on the version of Windows being used and the type of analysis being performed.

File system artifacts, registry artifacts, and user and system artifacts are three common types of artifacts that can be collected in digital forensics investigations.

1. **File system artifacts**: File system artifacts are pieces of data that are stored on a computer's file system. These artifacts can include files, folders, directories, and metadata such as file creation and modification timestamps. Examples of file system artifacts that can be analyzed in digital forensics investigations include file timestamps, deleted files, file metadata, and file content.

2. **Registry artifacts**: The Windows registry is a database that contains information about the configuration of a Windows operating system. Registry artifacts can include information about software installations, user activity, and system configurations. Examples of registry artifacts that can be analyzed in digital forensics investigations include user account information, application settings, and system configurations.

3. User and system artifacts: User and system artifacts are pieces of data that are generated by a computer system during normal use. These artifacts can include log files, event logs, and user activity logs. Examples of user and system artifacts that can be analyzed in digital forensics

investigations include login/logout times, file access times, and network connection logs.

By analyzing these types of artifacts, digital forensics investigators can reconstruct past events and potentially uncover evidence of criminal or malicious activity. It is important to note that the specific artifacts that can be collected and analyzed will depend on the type of system being investigated and the nature of the investigation.

One real-world scenario where collecting and analyzing Windows artifacts was used involved the investigation of an employee who was suspected of stealing confidential company data.

The employee's computer was seized and a forensic image of the hard drive was created. The forensic investigators then used specialized tools to collect and analyze Windows artifacts such as event logs, registry keys, and user account information.

Through the analysis of the artifacts, the investigators were able to identify several instances of the employee accessing and copying confidential files to external storage devices. The artifacts also showed that the employee had used a

USB device to bypass security measures and gain unauthorized access to restricted files.

The investigators also found evidence that the employee had attempted to cover their tracks by deleting files and browser history. However, through the use of forensic tools, the investigators were able to recover deleted files and identify the websites the employee had visited.

The analysis of the Windows artifacts was crucial in providing evidence of the employee's actions and building a case against them. It also demonstrated the importance of using specialized forensic tools to collect and analyze data from a computer in order to uncover suspicious activity and identify potential security breaches.

In this scenario, collecting and analyzing Windows artifacts was essential in identifying evidence of the employee's actions, determining the extent of the security breach, and helping the company take steps to prevent similar incidents from occurring in the future.

questions and answers

Q: What is the purpose of collecting and analyzing Windows artifacts? A: The purpose of collecting and analyzing Windows artifacts is to identify potential evidence of criminal or malicious activity on a computer system. By analyzing artifacts such as file system data, registry keys, and user activity logs, digital forensics investigators can reconstruct past events and potentially identify the source of a security breach or cyber attack.

Q: What are some common types of Windows artifacts that can be collected in digital forensics investigations? A: Some common types of Windows artifacts that can be collected in digital forensics investigations include file system data, registry keys, event logs, Internet history, email artifacts, memory artifacts, and user activity logs.

Q: What is the difference between volatile and non-volatile artifacts? A: Volatile artifacts are pieces of data that exist only in the computer's volatile memory (RAM) and are lost when the system is shut down or restarted. Non-volatile artifacts, on the other hand, are pieces of data that are stored on the computer's non-volatile storage media, such as the hard drive, and can be recovered even after the system is shut down.

Q: What is the importance of maintaining the integrity of Windows artifacts during a digital forensics investigation? A: Maintaining the integrity of Windows artifacts is critical in digital forensics investigations to ensure that the evidence collected can be admissible in court. If the integrity of the evidence is compromised, it may be inadmissible, and the investigation may be compromised. It is essential to use proper forensic procedures and tools to collect, analyze, and preserve Windows artifacts.

Q: What challenges may arise when collecting and analyzing Windows artifacts? A: Challenges that may arise when collecting and analyzing Windows artifacts include dealing with encrypted or password-protected files, identifying and interpreting artifacts that have been modified or deleted, and working with legacy or proprietary systems that may not be compatible with modern forensic tools and techniques. In addition, the sheer volume of data that can be collected from a Windows system can be overwhelming, making it challenging to identify and analyze relevant artifacts.

CHAPTER IV : WINDOWS FORENSIC TOOLS AND TECHNIQUES

Windows forensics is the process of collecting and analyzing digital evidence from Windows operating systems to reconstruct past events and identify potential security breaches or cyber attacks. There are many tools and techniques used in Windows forensics, including the following:

1. **Disk Imaging Tools:** Disk imaging tools are used to create an exact copy of a hard drive or storage media to ensure the integrity of the evidence. Examples of disk imaging tools include FTK Imager, Encase, and dd (a command-line tool in Linux).

2. **File Analysis Tools**: File analysis tools are used to analyze the contents of files on a Windows system. These tools can be used to identify malware, analyze file metadata, and recover deleted files. Examples of file analysis tools include Autopsy, The Sleuth Kit, and WinHex.

3. **Registry Analysis Tools**: Registry analysis tools are used to analyze the Windows registry database, which contains information about software installations, user activity, and system configurations. Examples of registry analysis tools include RegRipper and Windows Registry Analyzer (WRA).

4. **Memory Analysis Tools**: Memory analysis tools are used to analyze the contents of a computer's volatile memory (RAM) to identify malware, track user activity, and reconstruct past events. Examples of memory analysis tools include Volatility Framework and Rekall.

5. **Network Forensics Tools**: Network forensics tools are used to analyze network traffic to identify potential security breaches or cyber attacks. Examples of network forensics tools include Wireshark and Tcpdump.

6. **Live Forensics Tools**: Live forensics tools are used to analyze a running Windows system to identify malware or other security threats. Examples of live forensics tools include F-Response, Helix, and Redline.

In addition to these tools, digital forensics investigators may use a variety of techniques to collect and analyze digital evidence from Windows systems. These techniques may include keyword searches, timeline analysis, file carving, and hash analysis. It is important to use proper forensic procedures and tools to ensure the integrity of the evidence collected and to follow legal and ethical guidelines when conducting a digital forensics investigation.

key tools and techniques used in Windows forensics:

1. **Disk Imaging**: Disk imaging involves creating a forensic copy of a hard drive or storage media for analysis. This process preserves the original data and ensures that any analysis performed on the image does not alter the original evidence. Popular imaging tools include FTK Imager, Encase, and dd.

2. **Hashing**: Hashing involves creating a unique digital fingerprint of a file or image. This process verifies the integrity of the evidence and ensures that no changes have been made to the original data. Popular hashing tools include HashCalc, MD5summer, and SHA1sum.

3. **Analysis Tools**: Analysis tools are used to review the contents of a hard drive image, including file metadata, deleted files, and hidden data. Popular analysis tools include Autopsy, The Sleuth Kit, and Forensic Explorer.

4. Memory Analysis: Memory analysis involves examining the contents of a computer's RAM to uncover hidden data, malware, and evidence of cyber attacks. Popular memory analysis tools include Volatility Framework, Rekall, and Redline.

5. **Timeline Analysis:** Timeline analysis involves reconstructing the sequence of events on a computer to identify suspicious activity or security breaches. This technique involves examining file creation and modification dates, application logs, and other system data. Popular timeline analysis tools include Log2Timeline and Plaso.

6. **File Carving**: File carving involves searching for and extracting files from an image based on file headers and footers. This technique can help recover deleted files or identify hidden data. Popular file carving tools include Foremost and Scalpel.

These tools and techniques are used in conjunction with other digital forensics best practices to conduct a thorough

Q: What is disk imaging in Windows forensics?

A: Disk imaging is the process of creating a bit-by-bit copy of a hard drive or storage media for forensic analysis. This ensures that any analysis performed on the image does not alter the original evidence and preserves the integrity of the data.

Q: What is hashing in Windows forensics?

A: Hashing is the process of creating a unique digital fingerprint of a file or image. This fingerprint, known as a hash value, can be used to verify the integrity of the evidence and ensure that no changes have been made to the original data.

Q: What are some popular Windows forensic analysis tools?

A: Some popular Windows forensic analysis tools include Autopsy, The Sleuth Kit, Forensic Explorer, and X-Ways Forensics. These tools can be used to analyze file metadata, recover deleted files, and uncover hidden data on a Windows system.

Q: What is timeline analysis in Windows forensics?

A: Timeline analysis involves reconstructing the sequence of events on a Windows system to identify suspicious activity or security breaches. This technique involves examining file creation and modification dates, application logs, and other system data to identify potential threats.

CHAPTER V: CASE STUDIES

Windows forensics concepts and techniques can be applied in various real-world scenarios, including:

1. **Incident Response**: Windows forensics can be used in incident response investigations to identify the cause of a security breach and the extent of damage. This can involve analyzing system logs, memory dumps, and other artifacts to determine what happened on the system and when.

2. **Intellectual Property Theft**: Windows forensics can be used to investigate cases of intellectual property theft, such as when an employee steals company data. Forensic analysis can help determine how the data was stolen, who was responsible, and where it was taken.

3. **Employee Misconduct**: Windows forensics can be used to investigate cases of employee misconduct, such as when an employee engages in inappropriate behavior on company systems. Forensic analysis can help identify the employee and the scope of their actions.

4. **Fraud Investigations**: Windows forensics can be used to investigate cases of fraud, such as when financial records are altered or deleted. Forensic analysis can help determine who was responsible and the extent of the fraud.

5. **Cybercrime**: Windows forensics can be used to investigate cases of cybercrime, such as when a system is hacked or infected with malware. Forensic analysis can help identify the source of the attack and the damage it caused.

Overall, the application of Windows forensics concepts and techniques in real-world scenarios can help investigators understand what happened on a system, who was responsible, and what damage was done. This information can be used to prevent similar incidents from occurring in the future and to hold responsible parties accountable for their actions.

One real-world scenario where Windows forensics was used involves the investigation of a data breach at a large retail company.

The company discovered that their customer database had been compromised and sensitive information such as names, addresses, and credit card numbers had been stolen. The company engaged a team of forensic investigators to determine the cause of the breach and the extent of the damage.

The investigators began by collecting and analyzing data from the company's Windows-based servers and workstations. They focused on the logs generated by the servers, which contained information about user activity, system events, and network traffic.

The investigators used specialized forensic tools to examine the logs and identify any suspicious activity. They also analyzed memory dumps and file system artifacts to determine what files had been accessed and modified.

Through this analysis, the investigators were able to determine that the breach had occurred through a vulnerability in the company's payment processing system. They also discovered that the attacker had gained access to the system through a phishing email that had been sent to an employee.

The investigators were able to identify the attacker by tracing the IP address used to access the system and by analyzing other indicators of compromise. They then worked with law enforcement to apprehend the attacker and recover the stolen data.

In this scenario, the application of Windows forensics concepts and techniques was crucial in identifying the cause of the breach, the extent of the damage, and the perpetrator. It also helped the company take steps to prevent similar breaches from occurring in the future.

GLOSSARY

1. Digital Forensics - the process of collecting, preserving, and analyzing electronic data in a way that maintains its integrity and reliability for use as evidence in legal proceedings.

2. File System - a method used by operating systems to organize and store files on a computer's hard drive.

3. Metadata - information about a file that is stored in the file system and provides details such as the file name, creation date, and size.

4. Hash Value - a unique numerical value that is generated by a hashing algorithm and used to verify the integrity of data.

5. Imaging - the process of creating a forensic image of a hard drive or storage device for analysis.

6. Chain of Custody - the documentation and tracking of the location and handling of evidence from the time it is collected until it is presented in court.

7. Timeline Analysis - the process of reconstructing a chronological sequence of events based on the analysis of system logs and other forensic artifacts.

8. Registry - a database used by Windows to store system and application settings and configurations.

9. Keyword Search - the process of searching for specific keywords or phrases in a file or across a file system.

CONCLUSION

Windows forensics is a critical field that plays a vital role in the investigation of cybercrimes and security breaches. Forensic investigators use specialized tools and techniques to collect and analyze electronic data, identify suspicious activity, and build a case against perpetrators. The use of Windows forensic tools and techniques is essential in identifying the cause of a breach, the extent of the damage, and the perpetrators, and in helping organizations take steps to improve their security measures and prevent similar incidents from occurring in the future. Understanding the basic concepts and techniques of Windows forensics is essential for anyone involved in digital investigations or cybersecurity, as it provides a foundation for effective data collection, analysis, and interpretation.

www.ingramcontent.com/pod-product-compliance
Lightning Source LLC
Chambersburg PA
CBHW072147230526
45467CB00040B/775